Evan Price is a barrister with over 20 years' experience of disputes involving property, wills, trusts and estates. He practices from Ten Old Square in Lincoln's Inn and is a member of the STEP (the Society of Trusts and Estates Practitioners). He is regularly instructed to assist clients to resolve matters involving broad and knotty issues that require urgent assistance.

A Practical Guide to Challenging a Will Due to Undue Influence or Fraudulent Calumny

A Practical Guide to Challenging a Will Due to Undue Influence or Fraudulent Calumny

Evan Price
Barrister, Middle Temple

Law Brief Publishing

Published 2022 by Law Brief Publishing, an imprint of Law Brief Publishing Ltd
30 The Parks
Minehead
Somerset
TA24 8BT

www.lawbriefpublishing.com

Paperback: 978-1-913715-68-7

For my pupil supervisors,

my clerks and my Dad

CONTENTS

CHAPTER ONE

INTRODUCTION

Many discussions about wills and inheritance should probably start by stating something that may not always appear that obvious: beneficiaries do not have a right to inherit material things; rather inheritance is a windfall. You cannot assume that you will inherit a parent's skills and abilities – and assuming that you will inherit their assets or wealth and basing your future financial planning on that assumption is potentially rather risky.

A will maker can decide to give nothing to relatives at all and that will be a decision that cannot be challenged, save in particular circumstances some of which are considered in this guide.

The words 'testator' and 'testatrix' are often used elsewhere, but in this guide, I will use the words 'will maker' to refer to the person making the will as it is neutral. In many of the judgments that I will refer to, the older language will be used.

When I am writing about the person who drafts the text of the will, I will use the words 'will writer'. In many cases, this will be someone who has professional qualification – a lawyer, financial advisor or a someone who has qualifications and membership of an organisation such as the Society of Will Writers. It may also be someone who has no qualifications at all.

Disputes about wills and estates are very often nasty in tone and content. They can be immensely personal, destabilising and even threatening. Challenges to what appear otherwise to be valid wills are usually based on five different types of claims: -

1. That the will was forged or fabricated;

2. That the will maker did not have the capacity to make the will at the time it was made;

3. That the will maker did not know or understand the will that was made;

4. That the will maker was unduly influenced into making the will; and

5. That the will was procured from the will maker by fraud or fraudulent calumny.

Forgery and fabrication occur when someone forges or fabricates the document that is presented as the will of the deceased. These claims fall outside the scope of this guide.

When it comes to undue influence and fraud, including fraudulent calumny, the personal animus and general nastiness of these disputes can reach extremes that often result in the breakdown of personal relationships that can never be repaired afterwards. The result is that these claims should not, if the personal relationships are important to the parties involved, be made lightly, easily or without careful consideration and an understanding of the potential consequences of them.

This book is intended to be a practical guide to how challenges to wills on the grounds of undue influence and fraudulent calumny can be brought, what the legal issues are that arise from such challenges and what evidence may be required to what degree in order to succeed in such challenges.

This book concerns the law in England and Wales and every attempt has been made to ensure that the law is current as at 1st November 2021.

Some things to remember

Wills are documents that are not easily defined – in simple terms they are a document in which the will maker sets out, while they are alive, what he or she would like to happen to their property after they have died. They can be simple documents, or very complicated documents.

Wills are, by their very nature, usually of no legal effect until after the will maker has died. An exception exists in the case of mutual wills: where two people make wills that are executed and after the death of one mutual will maker, the other, still alive, is obliged to keep to the mutual will that they have already executed. Disputes about mutual wills fall outside the scope of this guide too.

Detailed analysis of the issues that are set out in this introduction and their consequences go beyond the scope of this guide, but as you will read, some of these issues are also relevant to questions of undue influence and fraud and will be considered in more detail and in that context.

Testamentary freedom

When making a will, a will maker has complete testamentary freedom. In the words of one judge,

> "… a man has absolute dominion over his own property, and if he being in possession of his faculties thinks fit to

> make a capricious will, a harsh will, or a cruel will, you have no right to set it aside on that ground, for that would be interfering with the liberty which the law gives him and not to allow him to make his will."[1]

While this complete freedom has been constrained by provisions such as those found in the Inheritance (Provisions for Families and Dependants) Act 1975 and its predecessors, the essential freedom stated here remains good law and unless and until there is a challenge to the will, the will maker can leave their property pretty much as they wish.

Many continental and other jurisdictions do not adopt this freedom and some care needs to be exercised when dealing with assets, particular land and real property, in those jurisdictions, even where the will maker was domiciled and resident in England and Wales and where the will is being administered in England and Wales. When dealing with estates where there is land or real property in the EU, will makers and advisors must consider to the effect of the EU Succession Regulation[2]. This regulation has a very long name and is often referred to as Brussels IV. Further consideration of Brussels IV falls outside the scope of this guide.

Capacity

A will maker must have what lawyers call 'testamentary capacity' to make a will. In many older cases, this is referred to as a 'sound disposing mind'. A person without testamentary capacity is incapable of making a will. Even if that person recovers, the invalid

---

[1] Cresswell J, *Earl of Sefton and anr v Hopwood* (1858) 175 ER 860

[2] Regulation (EU) No 650/2012.

will remains invalid unless it is re-executed after recovery.[3] Where the person becomes incapable after making a valid will, the fact of that later loss of capacity will not mean that the valid will becomes invalid.[4]

Although increasingly irrelevant due to the passage of time, the reader should note that a will made after 1 January 1970 by people aged 18 and over are valid in law; however, valid wills made by people under 21 before 1 January 1970 and otherwise valid wills made at any time by individuals under the age of 18 (subject to a limited number of exceptions[5]) will not be valid in law.[6] Since that date, a valid will made on someone's 18th birthday will be valid in law.

The Mental Capacity Act 2005 does not, it appears, apply to wills (save for statutory wills made with the assistance of the court after 1 April 2007) and so I will not be dealing with these issues in this guide[7].

The will maker must be shown to have had testamentary capacity at the time the will or codicil was made[8]. This has been held to require that capacity both when the instructions are given and when the will is executed (signed and witnessed). The will may still be valid if it is drawn up on the basis of valid instructions when the

---

[3] *Bunter v Coke* (1707) 1 Salk 237, Willock v Noble (1875) LR 7 HL 580

[4] *Forse and Hembling's case* (1588) 4 Co Rep 60 b

[5] Servicemen and women on active service and seamen and women at sea

[6] Wills Act 1837, s.7

[7] *Re Walker, Walker v Badmin* [2015] WTLR 493

[8] *Re Wilkes dec'd, Wilkes v Wilkes* [2006] WTLR 1097

will maker was of sound mind and the execution is done at a time when the will maker understands that he or she is making a will in accordance with his or her instructions and in spite of the fact that he or she is not able to follow all of the provisions of the will[9].

To prove capacity, it will be necessary to show four things.

1. The will maker must understand that he or she is giving his or her property to 'one or more objects of his or her regard'.

2. The will maker must understand and recollect the extent of his or her property, although the precise nature and value of the property is not usually necessary.

3. The will maker must understand the nature and extent of the claims upon him or her both those he or she is including in the will and those being excluded.

4. No insane delusion can influence the will maker in disposing of property or bring about a disposal of his or her property which, if the will maker had been of sound mind, would not have been made.

These requirements are drawn from the judgment of Cockburn CJ in the case of *Banks v Goodfellow* (1870) LR 5 QB 549.

There is a presumption that a will maker was sane at the time they made the will[10], but if capacity is doubted, the burden to prove

[9] *Perera v Perera* [1901] AC 354

[10] *Wellesley v Vere* (1841) 2 Curt 917

capacity will be on the person seeking to prove and rely on the will (lawyers will say 'propounding' the will)[11].

Knowledge and approval

When the court considers a will being proved for probate, the person proving the will must be able to show that the will maker knew of the contents of the will and approved of them[12]. Usually, this is achieved by proving a duly executed will, but in some cases, the court will ask for further proof.

Where a professionally drafted will has been read over to the will maker, or the contents of the will have been brought to the will maker's attention in some other way, and the will is then duly executed, there is a presumption of knowledge and approval, although in extreme circumstances, even that may not be enough.[13]

Where the will maker is deaf and dumb[14], or blind[15], and where the person who prepared the will received a benefit from it[16], the court will probably want more evidence that the will maker knew of and approved of the will.

---

[11] *Re Flynn, Flynn v Flynn* [1982] 1 All ER 882

[12] *Re Wilkes dec'd* (see note 7 above); *Re Baker, Baker v Baker* [2008] EWHC 937 (Ch)

[13] *Gill v Woodall* [2010] EWHC Civ 430

[14] *Dickinson v Blisset* (1754) 1 Dick 268

[15] *Fincham v Edwards* (1842) 3 Curt 63

[16] *Fulton v Andrew* (1875) LR 7 HL 448

Sometimes, facts are given that 'excite the suspicion' of the court[17]. These can include evidence of the relationship between the will maker and beneficiaries and those that prepare the will. In these cases, the court may wish to enquire further as to whether the will maker knew of and approved of the will.

Evidence and burden of proof

In many (if not all) claims challenging the will, both the capacity of the will maker and the knowledge and approval of the will maker will be raised. In these cases, there is a burden on the person seeking to prove and rely on the will to satisfy the court that the will is the last will of a free and capable testator[18].

In practice, where the will is duly executed, the court will assume, without more, that the will was the last will of a free and capable testator[19].

Where there are circumstances in which the court's suspicions are aroused, the person seeking to prove the and rely on the will must prove that the will maker had capacity and knew of and approved of the will. That the will did reflect the wishes of the deceased[20].

The standard of proof required by the court is the civil standard – on balance of probabilities[21]. The court may infer from the circumstances whether the will maker had capacity and whether the

---

[17] *Cowdery v Cranfield* [2011] EWHC 1616 (Ch)

[18] *Barry v Butlin* (1838) 2 Moo PCC 480

[19] *Fuller v Strum* [2001] EWCA Civ 1879, [2002] 1 WLR 1097

[20] *Fuller v Strum* (see note 18 above), per Peter Gibson LJ at p.1107

[21] *Fuller v Strum* (see note 18 above), per Chadwick LJ at p.1120

will maker knew of and approved of the will. The extent of the evidence that a court will require will inevitably depend on the seriousness of the evidence that is given to arouse the suspicion of the court.

There will be circumstances where the evidence to arouse the suspicion of the court will also be relevant to a plea of undue influence and fraud. As a result, it is often the case that the three claims are made simultaneously. Failing to plead undue influence and or fraud will not preclude the court examining that issue or finding that it is proved in an appropriate case.

Other books and guides deal with the issues of forgery and fabrication, mental capacity and want of knowledge and approval and anyone dealing with these issues should refer to those books and guides for more advice about challenging wills on those grounds.

CHAPTER TWO

UNDUE INFLUENCE

"While poor Mrs. Churchill lived, I suppose there could not have been a hope, a chance, a possibility; but scarcely are her remains at rest in the family vault, than her husband is persuaded to act exactly opposite to what she would have required. What a blessing it is, when undue influence does not survive the grave! He gave his consent with very little persuasion."

– Emma, Jane Austen, Chapter 10

What is it?

Undue influence is an equitable doctrine in the general law that applies to situations where transactions are procured by conduct, usually falling short of actual fraud, where one party seeks to use its position and influence to gain an unfair advantage over the other.

It applies to all sorts of transactions, commercial and personal and it will often involve someone who has a position of power or influence over the other. It is similar to the doctrine of duress in the sense that it will arise where one party has obtained the benefit of a transaction in circumstances where there is a lack of real consent and agreement by the other.

The reason that the courts recognise undue influence is that when they are considering the relationship between individuals, the courts should be concerned about the exploitation of people and their property by people who would otherwise be benefiting by that exploitation.

Lord Justice Mummery explained the objective of the undue influence doctrine as follows:

> "Although undue influence is sometimes described as an "equitable wrong" or even as a species of equitable fraud, the basis of the court's intervention is not the commission of a dishonest or wrongful act by the defendant, but that, as a matter of public policy, the presumed influence arising from the relationship of trust and confidence should not operate to the disadvantage of the victim, if the transaction is not satisfactorily explained by ordinary motives … The court scrutinises the circumstances in which the transaction, under which benefits were conferred on the recipient, took place and the nature of the continuing relationship between the parties, rather than any specific act or conduct on the part of the recipient. A transaction may be set aside by the court, even though the actions and conduct of the person who benefits from it could not be criticised as wrongful."[22]

There is a difference between the way in which the doctrine of undue influence can affect lifetime transactions and testamentary transactions.

Lifetime transactions

Lifetime transactions are transactions that deal with property (land, interests in land, money, financial instruments and all sorts of

[22] *Niersmans v Pesticcio* [2004] EWCA Civ 372, at §[20]

chattels and goods) that occur or are binding on the parties and made during the lifetime of both parties to the transaction. Testamentary transactions are transactions intended to have effect by a person after they have died.

Undue influence in relation to lifetime transactions has been the subject of court cases for very many years, but it was recently the subject of a comprehensive examination by the House of Lords in *Royal Bank of Scotland Plc v Etridge (No 2)* [2001] UKHL 44; [2002] 2 AC 773. I will refer to this case as the *Etridge* case or just *Etridge.*

In *Etridge*, the House of Lords had before it appeals in eight cases. Each case deal with a wife who jointly owned the family or matrimonial home with her husband. What had happened in each case was that the wife had agreed to charge (or mortgage) her interest in that home to the bank as security for her husband's borrowing or the borrowing of her husband's business. It was recognised that there were two forms of unacceptable conduct recognised as falling within the doctrine of undue influence.

> "The first comprises overt acts or improper pressure or coercion such as unlawful threats. The second form arises out of a relationship between two persons where one has acquired over another a measure of influence, as ascendancy, of which the ascendant person then takes unfair advantage."[23]

---

[23] *Etridge*, [2001] UKHL 44, [2002] 2 AC 773, 795C, per Lord Nicholls at §[8]

These two types of undue influence are often described as 'actual influence' and 'presumed undue influence'.

Actual undue influence

Where there is direct evidence of improper pressure or coercion applied to a person so as to overbear their free will in relation to a transaction, then that is described as 'actual undue influence'.

In *Bank of Credit and Commerce International SA v Aboody*[24], Slade LJ delivered the judgment of the Court of Appeal, explaining that,

> "… we think that a person relying on a plea of actual undue influence must show that (a) the other party to the transaction … had the capacity to influence the complainant; (b) the influence was exercised; (c) its exercise was undue; (d) that its exercise brought about the transaction."[25]

The court can find that actual undue influence occurred where there has been material misrepresentation or non-disclosure. In *Etridge*, Lord Nicholls explained that,

> "…where a husband, in whom a wife has reposed trust and confidence for the management of their financial affairs, prefers his interests to hers and makes a choice for them both on that footing. Such a husband abuses the confidence he has. He fails to discharge the obligation of candour and

[24] [1990] 1 QB 923

[25] [1990] 1 QB 923, at p.967

> fairness he owes a wife who is looking to him to make the major financial decisions."[26]

However, some care needs to be exercised, as,

> "[W]hen a husband is forecasting the future of his business, and expressing his hopes or fears, a degree of hyperbole may be only natural. Courts should not too readily treat such exaggerations as misrepresentations."[27]

The consequence of actual undue influence, where it is found to have occurred, is that the transaction can be reversed at the instance of the person who has been unduly influenced or someone acting on their behalf.

Presumed undue influence

This is the second of the two forms of unacceptable conduct described by Lord Nicholls in *Etridge*. It gives rise to a presumption, where a certain relationship exists between the influencer and the influenced, that undue influence will have occurred. This is an evidential presumption that can be rebutted by evidence to the contrary.

What happens is that the court will assume that the transaction has been unduly influenced and so is unfair, unless, on balance of probability, the evidence shows that there has been no such undue influence. The burden shifts to the party seeking to rely on the formality of the transaction.

[26] *Etridge*, supra, 800D at §[33]

[27] *Etridge*, supra, per Lord Nicholls, 800D, at §[32]

The presumption arises where two elements are established:

> "...the complainant reposed trust and confidence in the other party, or the party acquiring ascendancy over the complainant ..." and
>
> "...the transaction is not readily explicable by the relationship between the parties."[28]

There are certain relationships where the law provides that there is a legal presumption of influence which cannot be rebutted. This legal presumption does not result in an automatic finding that the influence was undue, but where it arises, the person who benefits from the transaction will have to show that they did not abuse the relationship or power that they had over the other party. The relationships that have been established as giving rise to this legal presumption include:

a. Solicitor and client.[29]

b. Trustee and beneficiary.[30]

---

[28] *Etridge*, supra, 797D, per Lord Nicholls at §[21]

[29] *Wintle v Nye* [1959] 1 WLR 284; *Etridge*, supra, 797 at §[18]; *AKB v Willerton* [2016] EWHC 3146 (QB), [2017] 4 WLR 25, at §[30]

[30] *Ellis v Barker* (1871) LR 7 Ch App 104; *Beningfield v Baxter* (1866) 12 App Cas 167

c. Parent and child.[31] This can extend to after the child reaches the age of majority[32]; after they marry[33]; but it depends on the facts and degree in the circumstances of an individual case.

d. Guardian and ward.[34]

e. Doctor and patient.[35]

The classes of relationships in which this legal presumption applies is not closed and changes over time.

The second part of the test is that the transaction is not readily explicable by the relationship between the parties. In *Etridge*, the House of Lords disapproved of idea that the transaction had to be to the 'manifest disadvantage' of the victim. This had been the position suggested in the case of *National Westminster Bank Plc v Morgan* [1985] AC 686; what is left is that the transaction calls of an explanation; it is one that does not easily fall to be explained by the relationship between the parties, their friendship, by charity or other ordinary motives that people may have[36].

---

[31] *Wright v Vanderplank* (1855) 2 Kay & J 1

[32] *Banbrigge v Browne* (1881) 18 Ch D 188; *re Pauling's Settlement Trusts* [1964] Ch 303, at p.336

[33] *Lancashire Loans Ltd v Black* [1934] 1 KB 380.

[34] *Hylton v Hylton* (1754) 2 Ves Sen 547

[35] *Mitchell v Homfrey* (1881) 8 QBD 587; *Radcliffe v Price* (1902) 18 TLR 466.

[36] Misquoting Lindley LJ in *Allcard v Skinner*, (1887) LR 36 Ch D 145, at p.185

Once the court is content that there is a relationship of trust of confidence giving rise to presumed undue influence, the burden to prove that the transaction was not obtained by that undue influence falls on the person benefiting from that transaction. That person must show that they did not abuse their position of trust and confidence.

Where there is a gift a small amount, the court will not set aside that gift simply on the ground that the donor had no independent advice. The greater the disadvantage, the more cogent the explanation must be before the presumption will be regarded as rebutted.[37]

Where the court is content that the influenced person has received competent and independent legal advice, the presumption will be rebutted. However, the involvement of a solicitor will not always be sufficient, rather,

> "It is necessary for the court to be satisfied that the advice and explanation by, for example, a solicitor, was relevant and effective to free the donor from the impairment of the influence on his free will and to give him the necessary independence of judgment and freedom to make choices with a full appreciation of what he was doing."[38]

Having written all of that, it is worth noting that in *Etridge*, Lord Clyde wrote:

> "At the end of the day, after trial, there will either be proof of undue influence or that proof will fail. and it will be

[37] *Etridge*, supra, 798G, §[24]

[38] *Niersmans v Pesticcio*, supra, at §[23]

found that there was no undue influence. In the former case, whatever the relationship of the parties and however the influence was exerted, there will be found to have been an actual case of undue influence. In the latter there will be none."[39]

[39] *Etridge*, supra, 816F, at §[93]

CHAPTER THREE

WILLS AND UNDUE INFLUENCE

The basics

For a will to be set aside on the ground of undue influence, there must be evidence of actual coercion.

What is required is that the will maker is coerced into making a will that the will maker would not otherwise have made[40].

It is necessary to show that the person relying on the will 'so overbore' the will maker's will 'as to induce him to make a will where he would not otherwise have done so.

In its most horrifying form, coercion will be violence, confinement or threatened violence that is sufficient to bring about the desired effect.

On the other hand, a really vulnerable person may be much more susceptible to pressure so that very little pressure, even simply talking to the will maker, is enough to overbear the will and cause the will maker to do anything to make the little pressure cease. In this case there will be coercion, even though there is no violence.

---

[40] *Wingrove v Wingrove* (1885) 11 PD 81

No presumption

There is no presumption of undue influence in the context of wills. In *Boyse v Rossborough*[41], the House of Lords decided that, in the case of a duly executed will, "undue influence cannot be presumed."

In *Craig v Lamoureux*[42], Lord Haldane reaffirmed that position and said,

> "... it is not sufficient to establish that a person has the power unduly to overbear the will of the testator. It must be show that in the particular case the power was exercised, and that it was by means of the exercise of that power that the will was obtained."[43]

If there is no coercion found by the court, then the challenge to the will on the grounds of undue influence will fail.

Persuasion is OK

Summarising undue influence in relation to a will, one judge said,

> "Persuasion is not unlawful, but pressure of whatever character if so exerted as to overpower the volition without convincing the judgment of the testator, will constitute

[41] (1857) 10 ER 1192, at p.1211

[42] [1920] AC 349

[43] *Craig v Lamoureux, supra*, at p.357

> undue influence, though no force is either used or threatened."[44]

So, it is often cryptically and somewhat unhelpfully said by tribunals considering undue influence claims that the will maker 'can be influenced but not unduly influenced'.

In *Edkins v Hopkins*[45], the court described the will maker as having acted as a free agent, but with the encouragement or even persuasion of the person who was his business partner and a significant beneficiary under the will. However, the court was satisfied that any such persuasion or encouragement did not "cross the line" so as to "rob [the will maker] of his judgment"[46].

What do you need to show?

In the case of *re Edwards (Deceased)*[47], Lewison J summarised the law in relation to undue influence rather concisely and neatly as follows:

> "i) In a case of a testamentary disposition of assets, unlike a lifetime disposition, there is no presumption of undue influence;

[44] Per Sir J P Wilde in *Hall v Hall* (1865-1869) LR 1 P&D 481 at p.482

[45] [2016] EWHC 2542 (Ch)

[46] *Edkins v Hopkins*, supra, at §[65]

[47] [2007] EWHC 1119 (Ch)

ii) Whether undue influence has procured the execution of a will is therefore a question of fact;

iii) The burden of proving it lies on the person who asserts it. It is not enough to prove that the facts are consistent with the hypothesis of undue influence. What must be shown is that the facts are inconsistent with any other hypothesis. In the modern law this is, perhaps no more than a reminder of the high burden, even on the civil standard, that a claimant bears in proving undue influence as vitiating a testamentary disposition;

iv) In this context undue influence means influence exercised either by coercion, in the sense that the testator's will must be overborne, or by fraud.

v) Coercion is pressure that overpowers the volition without convincing the testator's judgment. It is to be distinguished from mere persuasion, appeals to ties of affection or pity for future destitution, all of which are legitimate. Pressure which causes a testator to succumb for the sake of a quiet life, if carried to an extent that overbears the testator's free judgment discretion or wishes, is enough to amount to coercion in this sense;

vi) The physical and mental strength of the testator are relevant factors in determining how much pressure is necessary in order to overbear the will. The will of a weak and ill person may be more easily overborne than that of a hale and hearty one. As was said in one case simply to talk to a weak and feeble testator may so fatigue the brain that a sick person may be induced for quietness' sake to do

> anything. A "drip drip" approach may be highly effective in sapping the will;
>
> ...
>
> ix) The question is not whether the court considers that the testator's testamentary disposition is fair because, subject to statutory powers of intervention, a testator may dispose of his estate as he wishes. The question, in the end, is whether in making his dispositions, the testator has acted as a free agent."[48]

Every case will be different and will depend on its own unique set of circumstances and facts. Remember that there is no undue influence unless the will maker, if they could speak their wishes, would say, "this is not my wish but I must do it"[49].

Inferences drawn from facts

In *Schrader v Schrader*[50], it was accepted that the will was obtained by undue influence. The judge, Mann J said,

> "It will be a common feature of a large number of undue influence cases that there is no direct evidence of the application of influence. It is of the nature of undue influence that it goes on when no-one is looking. That does not stop its being proved. The proof has to come, if at all,

[48] *Re Edwards (Deceased)*, supra, at §[47]

[49] *Wingrove v Wingrove*, supra, at p.83

[50] [2013] EWHC 466 (Ch)

from more circumstantial evidence. The present case has those characteristics. The allegation is a serious one, so the evidence necessary to make out the case has to be commensurately stronger, on normal principles."[51]

The facts relied on by Mann J were as follows

a) The will maker was very elderly, vulnerable and in her 90's.

b) She was dependent on the defendant, who lived with her.

c) Her usual solicitors had not been used in making the will. Instead, a professional will writer, unfamiliar with the family, was instructed.

d) The reason that the will writer was given for leaving the house to the defendant was untrue and its source was likely to have been the defendant.

e) There was no other reason given for the will maker deciding to change her will and departing from pervious equal treatment of her sons (the claimant and the defendant).

f) The admitted forceful and physical presence of the defendant. No physical abuse or even real emotional abuse was found to exist, but the defendant was 'a powerful personality and his mother was much more vulnerable'.

g) The Defendant felt that he had been unfairly treated in the past and had a keen sense of entitlement as a result. He was 'inclined to even things up'.

[51] *Schrader v Schrader*, supra, at §[96]

h) The defendant tried to distance himself from consideration of the will, and from knowing what the will determined; and his failure to disclose the existence of the will under 6 months after his mother's death.[52]

It should be noted that *Schrader v Schrader* is an unusual case where undue influence was found, but claims relating to the deceased's capacity and an alleged want of knowledge and approval were rejected.

It should be noted that while the courts have accepted that undue influence can be found where there is no direct evidence of coercion and from inferences alone, the courts have not often decided that to be the case[53].

[52] *Schrader v Schrader*, supra, at §[97]

[53] See *Coles v Reynolds* [2020] EWHC 2151 (Ch); *Edkins v Hopkins* [2016] EWHC 2542 (Ch); contrast with *re Chin* [2019] EWHC 523 (Ch).

CHAPTER FOUR

FRAUDLUENT CALUMNY

"I'll pour this pestilence into his ear:

That she repeals him for her body's lust.

And by how much she strives to do him good

She shall undo her credit with the Moor.

So will I turn her virtue into pitch

And out of her own goodness make the net

That shall enmesh them all."

– Per Iago, Othello, Act 2, Scene 3

What is it?

This rare claim comes from the idea that a person can poison the will maker's mind against someone who would otherwise benefit from the will maker's will so that the will that is then made deprives the other person of that benefit. Fraudulent calumny is another form of fraud.

In essence, the false representations are made to the will maker and are intended to persuade the will maker to revoke a bequest or to exclude the other person from benefiting from the will[54].

The evidence supporting this claim is often part of the evidence that supports a claim of undue influence or a claim that that the will maker did not know of or approve of the contents of the will.

What do you need to show?

In *re Edwards (Deceased)*[55], Lewison J described the claim in this way:

> "vii) There is a separate ground for avoiding a testamentary disposition on the ground of fraud. The shorthand used to refer to this species of fraud is "fraudulent calumny". The basic idea is that if A poisons the testator's mind against B, who would otherwise be a natural beneficiary of the testator's bounty, by casting dishonest aspersions on his character, then the will is liable to be set aside;
>
> viii) The essence of fraudulent calumny is that the person alleged to have been poisoning the testator's mind must either know that the aspersions are false or not care whether they are true or false. In my judgment if a person believes that he is telling the truth about a potential beneficiary then

[54] See Lord Lyndhurst in *Allen v M'Pherson* (1847) 1 HLC 191; and see *White v White* (1862) 2 Sw & Tr 504

[55] [2007] EWHC 1119 (Ch)

> even if what he tells the testator is objectively untrue, the will is not liable to be set aside on that ground alone;"[56]

This formula was adopted by the judge in *re Hayward, Kunicki and anr v Hayward*[57], where he said that 'it was reasonable to suppose' that Lewison J set out those principles from 'the case of *Boyse v Rossborough*'[58].

In *Boyse v Rossborough* , Lord Cranworth, delivered the opinion (as Judgments in the House of Lords were called) and set out that: -

> "So as to fraud: if a wife by falsehood raises prejudices in the mind of her husband against those who would be the natural objects of his bounty, and by contrivance keeps him from intercourse with his relatives to the end that the impressions which she knows he has thus formed to their disadvantage may never be removed, such contrivance may, perhaps, be equivalent to positive fraud and may render invalid any will executed under false impressions thus kept alive. It is, however, extremely difficult to state in the abstract what acts will constitute undue influence in questions of this nature. It is sufficient to say that, allowing a fair latitude of construction, they must range themselves under one or other of these heads- coercion or fraud."

56 *Re Edwards (Deceased)*, supra, at §[47]

57 [2016] EWHC 3199 (Ch)

58 *Boyse v Rossborough*, supra, at 1211

An unusual claim

It is an unusual claim that, like undue influence, is sometimes raised with other challenges to a particular will.

In *re Boyes, Nesbitt v Nicholson and others*[59], a father's new will that disinherited his sons was held not to be invalid for undue influence by his daughter and his sons failed in their claim that the daughter had poisoned their father's mind against them by making false statements. Proudman J explained that the essence of fraudulent calumny was that the person alleged to have been poisoning the mind of the will maker had to either know that the aspersions were false or not care whether they were true or false. The judge accepted that the daughter had made the statements, but found that she believed them, wrongly or not.

In *Chistodoulides v Marcou*[60], one sister, Andre, sought to challenge the validity of her mother's will, which she claimed had been procured by the fraud practiced by her sister, Niki, on her mother. After a 10-day trial, the trial judge pronounced against the will on the grounds of fraudulent calumny. After a transaction which Niki objected to, Andre claimed that Niki accused Andre of taking or stealing large sums of money from their mother. When considering her evidence, the judge found that Niki was 'a thoroughly dishonest and manipulative individual to whom integrity and the truth are less important than achieving what she wants, even when she knows she is not entitled to it'[61]. Andre, by comparison, was 'calm and sensible' and 'dealt with all questions some of which were difficult

59 [2013] EWHC 4027 (Ch)

60 [2017] EWHC 2632 (Ch)

61 *Chistodoulides v Marcou*, supra, para [16]

and personal … in a convincing fashion'[62]. The trial judge had concluded that Niki had made allegations about a conspiracy to defraud her mother that were untrue and that she knew to be untrue; that she had made allegations about her sister's husband that were also untrue and which she knew to be untrue. He went on to conclude that their mother had believed the claims made by Niki and that she had altered her will based on them. An application for permission to appeal was refused on the ground that there was no real prospect of success.

In *Clitheroe v Bond*[63], a daughter sought to challenge her mother's wills that excluded her on grounds of lack of testamentary capacity and on grounds of fraudulent calumny. The mother had explained to the will writer that her daughter was a 'shopaholic and would just fritter it away' and that her daughter was a 'spendthrift and will just spend her inheritance'.[64] There was considerable evidence about the testamentary capacity of the deceased, including expert evidence and the judge decided that the mother did not have capacity at the time the wills were made. Having reached that decision, the judge considered whether there was fraudulent calumny and concluded that the sister had not discharged the burden on her to prove that the brother had encouraged their mother's incorrect beliefs and that the circumstantial evidence that had been given was not enough.

---

[62] *Chistodoulides v Marcou*, supra, para [17]

[63] [2020] EWHC 1185 (Ch)

[64] *Clitheroe v Bond*, supra, at §[11]

In *re Rea, Rea v Rea and others*[65], the will of Anna Rea was challenged by 3 of her children, who were defendants and who represented themselves at trial, on all of the grounds available, including fraudulent calumny. On appeal, Johnson J, explained that the defendants' claim of fraudulent calumny was 'closely related' to their undue influence claim and went on to say that 'fraudulent calumny … is a species of undue influence'[66]. The decision on appeal turned on grounds of fairness of the trial and the appeal was dismissed. A further appeal to the Court of Appeal is being considered at the time of writing this guide.

Contrast with knowledge and approval cases

These cases can be contrasted with cases where it is claimed that the deceased did not know of or approve of the contents of the will.

In *re Cole (Deceased), Middleton and ors v Boorman and anr*[67], the claimants and first defendant were siblings and children of the deceased. The second defendant was a firm of professional will writer, who was the executor of the estate. The claimants did not claim undue influence or fraudulent calumny and relied solely on a claim that the deceased did not know of or approve of the contents of the will. The claimants had, the judge concluded, been asked by their mother to administer their father's will on her behalf (their mother having been appointed executor). The judge expressed concern about the explanations given for things that the deceased appeared to rely on when explaining her instructions for the new

---

[65] [2021] EWHC 893 (Ch)

[66] *re Rea, Rea v Rea and others*, supra, para [16]

[67] [2020] EWHC 1481 (Ch)

will; and he concluded that the first defendant's son, Nicholas, 'did indeed put the idea that the Claimants had been up to no good into his grandmother's head or at the very lease encouraged any such thoughts which the Deceased may already have had'[68]. The judge considered what he described as the 'tug of war' between the sides of the family over bank accounts, over the recovery of documents and powers of attorney and expressed real concerns about the will writer's notes of the instructions given by the deceased in relation to the disputed will and concluded that the deceased did not know of or approve of the contents of the will.

A test

So, it may be that fraudulent calumny is merely a form of undue influence that arises in certain circumstances, or it may be that it is a separate claim[69]. For the purposes of this guide, to prove fraudulent calumny, the following factors will be required:

1. The person who is accused of the fraud has said something that is untrue;

2. The statement is made to the will maker;

3. The statement is about someone else who would otherwise be expected to benefit from the estate of the will maker;

[68] See para 71, [2020] EWHC 1481 (Ch)

[69] It is not necessary for this guide decide, but the author of this guide is of the view that they are similar but distinct claims and that it is not correct to describe fraudulent calumny as 'a species' of undue influence.

4. The statement is made to persuade or induce the will maker to change the will;

5. The person who made the untrue statement either knows that it is untrue or is reckless as to its truth; and

6. The will that is executed is in fact the result of the fraudulent calumny.

CHAPTER FIVE

OTHER THINGS TO THINK ABOUT

Claiming undue influence in relation to a will is discouraged[70]. Similarly, a court is unlikely to be very sympathetic to a claimant who claims fraudulent calumny lightly. It is like a claim of fraud and so should not be made easily. It should only be made where there is real evidence to support it.

As may be appreciated from this guide, every case where undue influence or fraudulent calumny has been claimed will necessarily depend on the evidence that is presented in relation to it.

Where might the evidence come from?

In most cases, the primary source of the evidence will be from the parties to the dispute and the witnesses who support them. These can include members of the deceased's family, neighbours, carers (whether professional or voluntary), and friends of the deceased and the parties.

In addition, where a professional will writer has been employed, that person (whether they are a solicitor or a member of another professional organisation) will almost certainly have taken detailed notes of their instructions and their impressions of the will maker at the time those instructions were given to them. They also should

70 See *Mitchell v Guard* (1863) 3 Sw & Tr 78; *Spiers v English* [1907] P 122

have retained copies of correspondence (whether notes of conversations in person or by telephone or copies of letters or emails to and from the deceased) which will all assist the court in understanding issues that may be relevant to claims of undue influence or fraudulent calumny.

Other evidence can come from contemporary documents such as diaries written by the deceased; evidence from witnesses who knew the deceased and heard of complaints by the deceased about the pressure they were under; or even from the general circumstances that existed at the time the will was made (as in *Schrader v Schrader*).

In this way, evidence about the personal conduct of the person who is alleged to have unduly influenced the will maker, can be relevant to issues of undue influence or fraudulent calumny. In *Schrader v Schrader*, the defendant had a history of violent outbursts and had even been arrested after a violent confrontation at a family wedding. In *Chistodoulides v Marcou*, Niki had a history of making untrue claims about her sister and her brother-in-law to third parties, including a bank; and even though the claims about the brother-in-law were distantly related to the case, they were of assistance to the Judge when considering the claim for fraudulent calumny.

Where a beneficiary of a will has also been involved in the preparation of the will, someone who wishes to challenge the will may be better advised to challenge the will on grounds of want of knowledge and approval, if there is no direct evidence of coercion[71].

---

[71] See *Wyniczenko v Plucinska-Surowka* [2005] EWHC 2794 (Ch) – a plea or forgery failed, the court deciding that there was a real possibility of forgery; but the will was set aside on grounds of want of knowledge and approval.

Having written that, there are many cases where the court has not accepted that there was undue influence, indeed undue influence has been disproved, but the court has still decided not to accept the will as having been proved[72].

In many cases, evidence from the deceased's GP or nursing staff proves helpful. Where there are claims regarding the capacity of the deceased to make a will, this evidence may be substantial; however, as explained elsewhere in this guide, this is merely part of the evidence that the court will consider and should not determine any particular issue.

Similarly, medical records may be considered relevant, and, in some cases, expert evidence will be required to assist the court to consider and interpret those records and their impact on the claims being made by the parties.

Where expert evidence is sought, Part 35 of the Civil Procedure Rules ('CPR') and the practice directions set out the process for obtaining that evidence, and the procedure to be followed by parties wishing to use expert evidence.

Further discussion about evidence appears in the chapter of this guide titled 'Practical Matters'.

Burden of proof

While the overall burden of proving the will lies on the person who seeks to rely on it (the person propounding the will), that burden is

---

[72] See *re Fuld (No 3),* supra; *Vaughan v Vaughan* [2002] EWHC 699 (Ch)

usually satisfied by showing the that will was duly executed and that the will maker had testamentary capacity.[73]

Once those formalities have been shown, then it is for the person claiming undue influence or fraudulent calumny to prove that claim. It is not enough to say that the circumstances in which the will was made are consistent with its having been procured by undue influence or fraudulent calumny, it must be shown that they are inconsistent with any other hypothesis[74].

The standard of proof

The standard of proof remains the civil standard of proof, although it is said that it requires more cogent evidence to satisfy a court on balance of probabilities where the claim is of fraud or undue influence in relation to a will[75].

---

[73] *Baker v Batt* (1838) 2 Moo PC 317; *Barry v Butlin* (1838) 2 Moo PC 480

[74] *Boyse v Rossborough*, supra, at p.1212

[75] See *re Edwards (Deceased)*, supra, at §[2]

CHAPTER SIX

PRACTICAL MATTERS

Introduction

In this chapter, it is proposed to deal with some of the issues that may arise in the course of investigating a claim of undue influence or fraudulent calumny and then address the practice of bringing the claim itself. This is intended to be a guide as to how to get from a position where a potential claimant is merely concerned about the circumstances in which a will came into being to the point at which a claim in which it is said that the will was procured by undue influence or fraudulent calumny is issued.

Non-contentious probate is the name used by the courts to describe the procedure by which wills are proved and where there is no dispute about the will that is being proved. It is, under the terms of the Administration of Justice Act 1970, dealt with by Family Division of the High Court.

A probate claim is any contentious claim that is made in connection with an application 'for ... the grant of probate ... or letters of administration ... [or] the revocation of such a grant ... or a decree pronouncing for or against the validity of an alleged will' which is not a claim which is non-contentious probate business.[76].

[76] See CPR rule 57.1(2)(a)

Any claim that is made that seeks to set aside a will on the ground of undue influence or fraudulent calumny is a probate claim and as such it is assigned to the Chancery Division of the High Court.

The procedure for any probate claim is governed by Part 57, CPR and care needs to be taken to ensure that the procedure is followed.

Limitation

There is no limitation period for probate claims. However, in *re Flynn (Deceased)*[77], Slade J observed that,

> "...the authorities cited to me ... tend to support the view that the court will never strike out an action to revoke a grant of probate or letters of administration on the mere ground of delay in instituting it, unless it is satisfied that the claim is otherwise frivolous or vexatious or is for other reasons an abuse of the process of the court."[78]

As a result, although it will not occur very often, it should be noted that a probate claim can be struck out for delay.

It has been held that, following the introduction of the CPR, there is no special rule applicable to probate cases based on a supposed sanctity of a grant of probate.

Where the court does consider the delay in a party bringing a claim or complying with an order of the court and the consequences of that delay or failure to comply, the court should 'do more than simply consider whether there had been an abuse'. The court

---

[77] [1982] 1 WLR 310

[78] *Re Flynn (Deceased)*, supra, p.318

should also consider 'the potentially adverse consequence of injustice and unfairness to a defendant, and whether there had been a disproportionate use of the court's resources'[79].

The result is that a party thinking about bringing a claim for undue influence or fraudulent calumny and which delays in bringing the claim can, in most cases, expect to be penalised in costs rather than have the claim struck out. There will be situations where failing to comply with directions, including previous costs orders, will result in the claim being struck out.

Who can bring a claim?

It is important to make sure that any potential claimant has standing or right or ability (lawyers may refer to this as *locus standi*) to bring the claim.

Part 57.7 of the CPR provides that a party to a probate claim must have an 'interest' in the estate.

All persons who can show that they have an interest in the estate or a possible interest in the estate and where the court has jurisdiction to make an order in a probate claim that may affect that interest or possible interest, however slightly, have a right to be a party to the claim[80].

In *Randall v Randall*[81], it was decided that the question of whether a party had a sufficient 'interest' was one a procedural question and

---

[79] Per Briggs J, *Wahab v Khan* [2011] EWHC 908 (Ch)

[80] See *Hingeston v Tucker* (1862) 2 Sw&Tr 596

[81] [2016] EWCA Civ 494, at [27]

that this ought to be given a broad meaning so as to give effect to the overriding objective of the CPR and in particular Part 1.1(1) of the CPR[82]. In *Randall v Randall*, it was held that a creditor of a beneficiary of the estate has a sufficient interest.

Others who may have a sufficient interest include the following:

1. anyone interested in the estate where there is no will if the will is revoked (what lawyers refer to as intestacy);

2. the executor or beneficiary under another will of the deceased[83];

3. a person who is entitled to apply for family provision[84];

4. where the deceased died without any known relatives and so the estate falls to be dealt with under the bona vacantia principles. In these cases, the claim would be brought by the Treasury Solicitor or by solicitors for the Duchy or Lancaster or Duchy of Cornwall.

There are other situations where someone might have sufficient interest in the estate to bring a probate claim, and some care will need to be taken to ensure that any potential claimant does indeed have a sufficient interest to bring the claim.

---

[82] *Randall v Randall*, supra, at [28]

[83] But if the claimant has also received a legacy under the will, then he may be required to pay that legacy into court pending resolution of the claim – see *Bell v Armstrong* (1822) 162 ER 129

[84] Their other claim would be under the Inheritance (Provision for Family and Dependants) Act 1975, *Re Seagrave, O'Brien v Seagrave* [2007] 1 WLR 2002

Privilege issues

Sometimes, potential claimants will find the lawyers, who represented the deceased and advised the deceased about the will that is being contested, asserting that the documents that the potential claimants seek are protected by legal privilege and so cannot bc disclosed to the potential claimant.

In essence, legal privilege is a concept that says that the lawyer and his client have a relationship that means that the communications between the lawyer and the client for the purpose of giving or receiving legal advice is protected from disclosure to third parties.

The death of a client does not terminate the relationship of privilege between a client and solicitor. As a result, the advice given to the deceased remains subject to legal privilege and so ought not to be disclosed to anyone who is not entitled to see it.

However, a claimant who is seeking to bring a claim on behalf of an estate (as beneficiaries of the estate), is a successor in title to the deceased and so legal privilege cannot properly be asserted against them[85].

As a result, someone who shows that they have an interest in the estate and claims that the will was procured by undue influence or fraudulent calumny is a person who is seeking to claim on behalf of the estate and, ordinarily, legal privilege cannot properly be asserted against them.

It should be noted, however, that a claimant who has not established that they are a beneficiary of an estate will not be

[85] *Birdseye v Roythorne & Co* [2015] EWHC 1003 (Ch)

entitled to privileged information[86]. This may result in discussion about the interest of the potential claimant which has already been dealt with in this guide.

In relation to claims of undue influence and fraudulent calumny, therefore, it is likely that the parties bringing the claim, will do so as beneficiaries or potential beneficiaries of the estate. So, their claims are likely to be said to be on behalf of the estate. As a result, it is unlikely that a claim to legal privilege will survive against them.

Where to start

Before a potential claimant starts to raise their claim, there are a number of things that they need to think about. Most will relate to evidence, but others will relate to the documents that will be needed by any potential claimant before they issue any proceedings.

Larke v Nugus[87]

Before any steps are taken to start a claim that the will has been obtained by undue influence or fraudulent calumny, it is good practice for potential claimants to write to any will writer and ask them to explain how the will came to be executed, what instructions were given for that will and the circumstances surrounding it. This has become known as a *Larke v Nugus* request and its name comes from a reported case in which it occurred.

---

[86] See *Birdseye v Raythorne & Co*, supra, [24] and *O'Rourke v Darbishire* [1920] AC 581

[87] *re Moss, Larke v Nugus* [2000] WTLR 1033

What should be included in a *Larke v Nugus* letter? These are some of the things that can be considered.

- Who was present when the will was executed? Where and when was it executed?

- Who wrote the will? How long did the will writer know the deceased?

- Who introduced the will writer to the deceased?

- When did the will writer receive instructions from the deceased? How were those instructions given to the will writer?

- Copies of any contemporaneous notes – meetings, telephone calls etc – should be asked for, including dates and times the meetings took place and who was present at the meeting.

- Did the deceased know that they were making a will and how did the will writer come to understand that that was the case?

- Did the deceased show any signs of confusion or loss or memory?

- Where there any discussions about earlier wills? What were the details of those discussions? Were there any attempts to discuss changes from earlier wills? To the extent that there were changes, what reasons did the deceased give for making those changes?

- How did the will writer explain the provisions of the will to the deceased?

Where undue influence is alleged, consideration should be given to asking additional questions relating to what the will writer knows or knew about the relationship between the deceased and the person who is claimed to have unduly influenced the deceased at the time the instructions were given.

Where a claim is for fraudulent calumny, questions relating to the will writers understanding about the deceased's views of the disappointed beneficiary can be considered. These may include questions about what the will writer understood were the reasons for the exclusion of a particular beneficiary.

In most cases, the response to the *Larke v Nugus* letter may provide considerable useful information to a potential claimant.

The 'Golden Rule' – which is not a rule at all

Where the deceased was elderly and frail when the contested will was executed, many professional will writers talk about the 'Golden Rule'; this refers to comments made by Templeman J in his decision of *Kenward v Adams*[88]. Templeman J further explained his 'rule' in *re Simpson*[89],

> "In the case of an aged testator or a testator who has suffered a serious illness, there is one golden rule which should always be observed, however straightforward matters may appear and however difficult or tactless it may be to suggest that

[88] The Times, 29 November 1975 (ChD), unreported

[89] (1977) 121 SJ 224

precautions may be taken: the making of a will by such a testator ought to be witnessed or approved by a medical practitioner who satisfied himself of the capacity and understanding of the testator, and records and preserves his examination and finding."

In *Hoff v Atherton*[90], Peter Gibson LJ said that *Kenward v Adams* was 'too briefly reported to be of much assistance' and noted that the Golden Rule 'does not purport to lay down the law', going on to say that the comments were 'prudent guidance for solicitors'.

In *re Key (Deceased)*[91], Briggs J said,

> "Compliance with the Golden Rule does not, of course, operate as a touchstone of the validity of a will, not does non-compliance demonstrate its invalidity. Its purpose, as has been repeatedly emphasised, is to assist in the avoidance of disputes, or at least the minimisation of their scope."

The result is that the 'Golden Rule' is not a rule at all; it is merely a statement of good practice.

As a result, if it is followed, it will form a part of the evidence that the court assesses and may well not resolve or even necessarily be relevant to the questions relating to undue influence and fraudulent calumny.

For example, in a case where fraudulent calumny is claimed, the person who follows the Golden Rule may not have any knowledge of the party challenging the will and so may not be in a position to

---

[90] [2004] EWCA Civ 1554

[91] [2010] EWHC 408 (Ch)

make any assessment of the validity of the claimed reasons for the new will and the reasons why a particular beneficiary of earlier wills is now being excluded.

However, where the deceased was elderly and vulnerable when the contested will was executed, a person seeking to challenge the validity of the will on the grounds of undue influence or fraudulent calumny may wish to ask quite detailed questions about any decision not to follow the 'Golden Rule'[92].

In *Todd v Parsons*[93], the solicitor had not complied with the 'golden rule'[94] and the Judge expressly decided that this did not demonstrate invalidity following the decision in *re Key (Deceased)*[95]. The

Testamentary documents

There can be argument about whether the potential claimant should have access to the documents that relate to the will that is being disputed. These documents are called the 'testamentary documents' and are sometimes referred to as the 'script'.

[92] It may be interesting to note that Lord Templeman's own estate was challenged and despite the will being settled after he had clearly been suffering from issues relating to his own mental capacity, the solicitor who drafted the will did not follow the 'Golden Rule'; it appears for fear of offending his client! See re Baron Templeman (Deceased) [2020] EWHC 632 (Ch)

[93] [2019] EWHC 3366 (Ch)

[94] See para [135], [2019] EWHC 3366 (Ch)

[95] [2010] EWHC 408 (Ch)

A testamentary document is defined in Part 57.1(2)(c) of the CPR as follows:

> "a will, a draft of a will, written instructions for a will made by or at the request of, or under the instructions of, the testator, and any document purporting to be evidence of the contents, or a copy, of a will which is alleged to have been lost or destroyed."

As will be understood from that text, the class of documents that is included in that definition is widely defined.

Where someone refuses to disclose or allow someone else to inspect or have a copy of a testamentary document or documents, the courts have power, pursuant to s.123, Senior Courts Act 1981, to order a person holding a document to 'bring it in' to the court.

This would be a court order that requires a party who is believed to hold such documents to take them to the Principal Registry of the Family Division or into a district probate registry as the court may direct.

If there are no current proceedings, this is done by a without notice application for a subpoena in the Principal Registry or district probate registry. The application must be supported by an affidavit or a witness statement – see rule 50(2), Non-Contentious Probate Rules 1987 (as amended).

The evidence in support will set out the standing of the person making the application in respect of the estate and will set out the reasons why that person is asking for the court order.

It will include an explanation of what documents are being sought, and why the person who is the subject of the application is thought to have those documents in their possession, custody or control.

If the court makes an order, then the order must be served personally on the person to whom it is directed. In addition, it must include a penal notice[96].

It is doubted that any such subpoena can be issue for service outside the jurisdiction.

Once served, the person subject to the subpoena must bring the 'script' in their possession or control into court of, if they do not have the 'script' in their possession or control, they should file an affidavit or witness statement in the relevant court to that effect.

A solicitor cannot exercise a lien over the 'script'. This is a claim that fees have not been paid justifying a refusal to bring the 'script' into court until they have been paid[97].

If the arguments about these documents continue, then s.122, Senior Courts Act 1981 provides that where it is believed that a person has knowledge of a 'script', but they are not making a statement on the matter or are making one that appears to be

[96] Part 37.2 of the CPR defines a penal notice as "a prominent notice on the front of an order warning that if the person against whom the order is made (and, in the case of a corporate body, a director or officer of that body) disobeys the court's order, the person (or director or officer) may be held in contempt of court and punished by a fine, imprisonment, confiscation of assets or other punishment under the law."

[97] *Georges v Georges* (1811) 18 Ves 294

misleading or is deliberately incomplete, then an application can be made for an oral examination of that person[98].

Any such examination takes place on a date fixed for the attendance of the person summoned by the subpoena and that person will be cross-examined by the applicant's advocate.

Preventing probate being granted – the caveat

A caveat is a notice in writing that no grant of probate or letters of administration is to be sealed in the estate of a named deceased, without notice to the person who has given that notice. The process for caveats is governed by rule 44, Non-Contentious Probate Rules 1987 (as amended)[99].

Once a caveat has been entered, no grant of probate or letters of administration can be sealed, save for limited grants which are granted for specific purposes usually to protect assets of the estate and with no power to distribute any of those assets to beneficiaries pending suit[100]. Where a grant has already been obtained or is sealed on the day on which the caveat is entered, then the caveat will have no effect.

In the context of a person seeking to claim that a will has been obtained by undue influence of fraudulent calumny, it may well be

---

98 Rule 50(1), Non-Contentious Probate Rules 1987

99 These rules are the subject of proposals for reform and have been so since new draft Probate Rules were published in 2013. Under these new draft rules, caveats will be replaced by objections and the procedure will change under new draft rules 55-60.

100 Rule 44(1), Non-Contentious Probate Rules 1987

sensible, if not probate or letters of administration have been obtained, for the potential claimant to slow the process down by applying for a caveat in respect of the deceased's estate.

At the time of writing this guide, a caveat can be applied for: -

- online[101] or
- by completing a form[102] and sending it to the relevant court office[103].

A fee is payable on the application[104], and the caveat lasts for 6 months from the date on which it is entered[105], although it can be extended by an application made within the last month of the 6-month period, for an additional 6 months[106], and for further 6-month periods by successive applications, subject to the same conditions as the first extension[107].

---

[101] https://www.gov.uk/stop-probate-application

[102] At the time of writing, this is Form PA8A

[103] At the time of writing, the address is HMCTS Probate, PO Box 12625, Harlow CM20 9QE

[104] At the time of writing, £3

[105] Rule 44(3)(a), Non-Contentious Probate Rules 1987

[106] Rule 44(3)(b), Non-Contentious Probate Rules 1987

[107] Rule 44(3)(c), Non-Contentious Probate Rules 1987

A person who has an interest in the estate can set out their objection to the caveat in a document called a warning[108]. The warning is in a form that is required to be used[109].

The warning requires the person who has entered the caveat to respond[110] to the warning within 8 days of the warning. Any response by the person who has entered the caveat should: -

- set out the interest of the person who has entered the caveat in the estate of the deceased which is contrary to the interest of the person who has objected to the caveat, or

- if the person with the caveat objects to the sealing of the grant of probate, issue and serve in those 8 days, a summons returnable before a registrar[111].

If the person with the caveat does not 'enter an appearance', the court may make a grant of probate notwithstanding the caveat. The 'appearance' is also done in a form that is required to be used[112].

Assuming that there is a genuine claim of undue influence or fraudulent calumny, the caveat will remain in force until the commencement of the probate claim in which that claim is made.

108 Rule 44(5), Non-Contentious Probate Rules 1987

109 Rule 44(5) and Form 4, Sched 1, Non-Contentious Probate Rules 1987

110 In the language of the rules, 'to enter an appearance'

111 Rule 44(6), Non-Contentious Probate Rules 1987

112 Form 5, Sched 1, Non-Contentious Probate Rules 1987

The person who has entered the caveat may, before entering an appearance to the warning, withdraw his caveat; however, if the caveat has been warned, he must give notice of the withdrawal to the person who has warned it.[113].

Any caveat that is effective will remain in force (unless the court orders otherwise or it is withdraw) until a court order is made in the probate action[114].

Letter of claim or letter before action

Currently, there is no specific pre-action protocol for probate disputes, so the CPR Pre-Action Conduct and Protocols apply[115]. These are processes that the court will expect the parties to have complied with before any proceedings are commenced.

Another source of guidance is to be found in Practice Guidance Notes for the Resolution of Trust and Probate Disputes produced by the Association of Trusts and Estates Practitioners[116] ('ACTAPS').

When all the available evidence has been gathered by a potential claimant, the next step is to prepare a letter of claim. This is a letter that sets out the claim that is being made and asks the person to

---

[113] Rule 44(11), Non-Contentious Probate Rules 1987

[114] Rule 45(3), Non-Contentious Probate Rules 1987

[115] https://www.justice.gov.uk/courts/procedure-rules/civil/rules/pd_pre-action_conduct

[116] https://actaps.com/prelimininary-note/

whom it is addressed to do the thing or things that the claimant requires to be done, or else.

The letter of claim should set out: -

- concise details of the claim;
- the basis of which the claim is made;
- a summary of the facts relied on;
- what the claimant wants from the person to whom the letter of claim is addressed; and
- if there is a claim for money, the sum required and how that is calculated.

The letter of claim is not equivalent to a formal case (statement of case or pleading) as prepared for court. Indeed, it should be noted that a letter of claim may receive a response that substantially alters the case that is then the subject of the claim in court.

A reasonable time should be allowed for a response. A minimum of 14 days and a maximum of 3 months is suggested as a general guide, but the complexity of the case, the history being considered and the difficulties that may be encountered when seeking evidence will affect the time needed. In cases where undue influence and fraudulent calumny are claimed, it is suggested that more time is provided, as the history will often be quite detailed, and evidence is not always easy to obtain.

All the key documents should be disclosed with the letter of claim.

In a claim where undue influence or fraudulent calumny is claimed, it is possible that the remedy sought will be that the will that was produced because of the claimed undue influence or fraudulent calumny should not be proved and that an earlier will, untainted by that undue influence or fraudulent calumny, should be proved in its place. Alternatively, it may be that an intestacy will follow, there being no earlier will capable of being proved.

If the will has already been proved, then the possible remedy that will be sought is that the court will order that will, tainted by undue influence or fraudulent calumny, will be pronounced against and an earlier will proved in it place.

The claim in court

Assuming that the parties have not been able to reach a settlement between them, the next step in bringing a claim for undue influence or fraudulent calumny will be to issue the claim itself.

A probate claim follows the procedure set out in Part 7 of the CPR[117].

Part 64.4 of the CPR provides that: -

(a) "all the trustees must be parties;

(b) …

(c) The claimant may make parties to the claim any persons with an interest in or claim against the estate … who it is

[117] CPR Part 57(3)(b)

appropriate to make parties having regard to the nature of the order sought."

It is suggested that anyone who is a beneficiary of the estate under the terms of the disputed will and whose interest would be affected by the claim should be joined as a party to the claim. In addition, anyone who would have an interest in the estate as dealt with earlier in this guide, should be a party to the clam.

The court can order additional persons to be made parties to the claim under CPR Part 19.2 if necessary.

Where there is a person interested in the estate who is a child or who lacks capacity to conduct proceedings (for example, is elderly and is unable to look after their own affairs), then the person seeking to bring the claim must consider making an application under CPR Part 21 for the court to appoint a 'litigation friend'.

When the claim is issued, no probate can be granted until after the court makes an order on the claim[118].

The claim form[119] must include the name of the deceased as well as the name of the parties. The form required is "In the estate of [*name of the deceased*] deceased (Probate)"[120].

---

[118] Rule 45(1), Non-Contentious Probate Rules 1987

[119] Form N2

[120] See para 2.1m CPR PD 57A

The claim form must contain a statement setting out the nature of the interest of the claimant and each defendant in the estate[121].

This means, for example, that if the Claimant is a potential beneficiary on intestacy, then this should be recorded on the claim form; if a Defendant is appointed as executor in a disputed will, then this should also be recorded. Where someone has entered a caveat, then this information should also be included.

The claimant must prepare a document which sets out the facts of the case that is being made. This is called the Particulars of Claim and there are detailed rules for these documents in Part 16.4 of the CPR. There is also guidance in the Chancery Guide that ought to be considered.

The Particulars of Claim should be included with the claim form or served on the defendants within 14 days after service of the claim form[122].

Testamentary Documents – again

Part 57.5(1) of the CPR provides that all parties must lodge with the court any testamentary documents that they have in their possession or control. A claimant must do this when the claim form is issued[123], and any defendant must do this when they acknowledge service of the claim[124].

---

[121] CPR Part 57.7

[122] CPR Part 7.4

[123] CPR Part 57.5(2)(a)

[124] CPR Part 57.5(2)(b)

The testamentary documents must be in the form of written evidence[125] and this usually takes the form of a witness statement which is to be made by the party personally (not their lawyer), unless they are a protected party or child (when the evidence is provided by their litigation friend).

There is a specimen for the written evidence in the practice direction to Part 57A.

No-one can inspect the evidence of testamentary documents of another party or the testamentary documents themselves until they have filed their own evidence of testamentary documents, except with permission of the court[126].

In most cases when a person is bringing a claim for undue influence or fraudulent calumny, they will not be concerned about providing the testamentary documents to the other side as these will have already been copied to all parties in advance of the pre-action correspondence. However, where there remain questions about the interest of a particular claimant, the estate may still require the claimant to file their testamentary documents before allowing them to inspect the testamentary documents of the estate.

The Defendants' responses

Anyone served with a claim form is required to file an acknowledgment of service[127] and when filing that

[125] CPR Part 57.1(3)

[126] CPR Part 57.5

[127] CPR Part 57.4

acknowledgment, it has already been noted that any defendant should also file their testamentary documents[128].

Where the claim form is served with the Particulars of Claim, the time for filing the acknowledgment of service is 28 days after service of the claim form[129]. Where the claim form is served and the Particulars of Claim are served afterwards, then the time for filing the acknowledgement of service is 28 days after service of the Particulars of Claim[130].

Where there is no response to the Claim, there is no power in the court to order what is known as a default judgment[131]; if any of several defendants fails to acknowledge service, then the claimant may proceed as if that defendant had acknowledged service[132] if the claimant has filed written evidence of service of the claim form and particulars of claim.

If there is no response from any defendant, then the Claimant can seek to discontinue the claim or seek to have the claim proceed to trial[133]. Where the claim is for undue influence or fraudulent calumny, the Claimant will want the matter to proceed to trial so that they can formally prove their case.

When making the application for the claim to proceed to trial where there has been no acknowledgment from any defendant, the

---

[128] CPR Part 57.5(2)(b)

[129] CPR Part 57.4(2)(b)

[130] CPR Part 57.4(2)(a)

[131] CPR Part 57.10(1)

[132] CPR Part 57.10(2)

[133] CPR Part 57.10(3)

Claimant will have to prove that they have served the claim and particulars of claim (if served separately)[134]; and in that case, the court may order the matter to be tried on written evidence[135].

Some thoughts about costs

Litigation costs in general fall outside the scope of this guide, but it is important for anyone bringing a claim for undue influence or fraudulent calumny to know that in England & Wales, litigation is very expensive. It would be normal for each party to a probate claim where the issues are undue influence or fraudulent calumny to spend many thousands (and in some cases tens of thousands) on their case before any trial takes place.

The costs of any claim are in the direction of the court; and usually, the costs of a claim for undue influence or fraudulent calumny will be borne by the losing party[136]. However, there are a number of additional factors that will need to be thought about.

A professional executor will ordinarily be entitled to their costs from the estate if they simply respond to the claim by saying that they take a neutral stand between the competing beneficiaries and that they will abide by the decision of the court. However, if the executor decides to do more than take a neutral stand, and 'enter the fray' then their costs will follow the usual rules.

---

134 CPR Part 57.10(4)

135 CPR Part 57.10(5)

136 The costs will 'follow the event'

MORE BOOKS BY LAW BRIEF PUBLISHING

A selection of our other titles available now:-

'A Practical Guide to Transgender Law' by Robin Moira White & Nicola Newbegin
'Artificial Intelligence – The Practical Legal Issues (2nd Edition)' by John Buyers
'A Practical Guide to Challenging Sham Marriage Allegations in Immigration Law' by Priya Solanki
'A Practical Guide to New Build Conveyancing' by Paul Sams & Rebecca East
'A Practical Guide to Inherited Wealth on Divorce' by Hayley Trim
'A Practical Guide to Shareholder Disputes in Family Businesses' by Ed Weeks
'A Practical Guide to the Law of Forests in Scotland' by Philip Buchan
'A Practical Guide to Health and Medical Cases in Immigration Law' by Rebecca Chapman & Miranda Butler
'A Practical Guide to Bad Character Evidence for Criminal Practitioners by Aparna Rao
'A Practical Guide to Environmental Enforcement' by Christopher Badger & Stuart Jessop
'A Practical Guide to Hoarding and Mental Health for Housing Lawyers' by Rachel Coyle
'A Practical Guide to Psychiatric Claims in Personal Injury – 2nd Edition' by Liam Ryan
'Stephens on Contractual Indemnities' by Richard Stephens
'A Practical Guide to the EU Succession Regulation' by Richard Frimston
'A Practical Guide to Solicitor and Client Costs – 2nd Edition' by Robin Dunne
'Constructive Dismissal – Practice Pointers and Principles' by Benjimin Burgher
'A Practical Guide to Religion and Belief Discrimination Claims in the Workplace' by Kashif Ali
'A Practical Guide to the Law of Medical Treatment Decisions' by Ben Troke

'Fundamental Dishonesty and QOCS in Personal Injury Proceedings: Law and Practice' by Jake Rowley
'A Practical Guide to the Law in Relation to School Exclusions' by Charlotte Hadfield & Alice de Coverley
'A Practical Guide to Divorce for the Silver Separators' by Karin Walker
'The Right to be Forgotten – The Law and Practical Issues' by Melissa Stock
'A Practical Guide to Planning Law and Rights of Way in National Parks, the Broads and AONBs' by James Maurici QC, James Neill et al
'A Practical Guide to Election Law' by Tom Tabori
'A Practical Guide to the Law in Relation to Surrogacy' by Andrew Powell
'A Practical Guide to Claims Arising from Fatal Accidents – 2nd Edition' by James Patience
'A Practical Guide to the Ownership of Employee Inventions – From Entitlement to Compensation' by James Tumbridge & Ashley Roughton
'A Practical Guide to Asbestos Claims' by Jonathan Owen & Gareth McAloon
'A Practical Guide to Stamp Duty Land Tax in England and Northern Ireland' by Suzanne O'Hara
'A Practical Guide to the Law of Farming Partnerships' by Philip Whitcomb
'Covid-19, Homeworking and the Law – The Essential Guide to Employment and GDPR Issues' by Forbes Solicitors
'Covid-19, Force Majeure and Frustration of Contracts – The Essential Guide' by Keith Markham
'Covid-19 and Criminal Law – The Essential Guide' by Ramya Nagesh
'Covid-19 and Family Law in England and Wales – The Essential Guide' by Safda Mahmood
'A Practical Guide to the Law of Unlawful Eviction and Harassment – 2nd Edition' by Stephanie Lovegrove
'Covid-19, Residential Property, Equity Release and Enfranchisement – The Essential Guide' by Paul Sams and Louise Uphill
'Covid-19, Brexit and the Law of Commercial Leases – The Essential Guide' by Mark Shelton
'A Practical Guide to Costs in Personal Injury Claims – 2nd Edition' by Matthew Hoe

'A Practical Guide to the General Data Protection Regulation (GDPR) – 2nd Edition' by Keith Markham
'Ellis on Credit Hire – Sixth Edition' by Aidan Ellis & Tim Kevan
'A Practical Guide to Working with Litigants in Person and McKenzie Friends in Family Cases' by Stuart Barlow
'Protecting Unregistered Brands: A Practical Guide to the Law of Passing Off' by Lorna Brazell
'A Practical Guide to Secondary Liability and Joint Enterprise Post-Jogee' by Joanne Cecil & James Mehigan
'A Practical Guide to the Pre-Action RTA Claims Protocol for Personal Injury Lawyers' by Antonia Ford
'A Practical Guide to Neighbour Disputes and the Law' by Alexander Walsh
'A Practical Guide to Forfeiture of Leases' by Mark Shelton
'A Practical Guide to Coercive Control for Legal Practitioners and Victims' by Rachel Horman
'A Practical Guide to Rights Over Airspace and Subsoil' by Daniel Gatty
'Tackling Disclosure in the Criminal Courts – A Practitioner's Guide' by Narita Bahra QC & Don Ramble
'A Practical Guide to the Law of Driverless Cars – Second Edition' by Alex Glassbrook, Emma Northey & Scarlett Milligan
'A Practical Guide to TOLATA Claims' by Greg Williams
'A Practical Guide to Elderly Law – 2nd Edition' by Justin Patten
'A Practical Guide to the Law of Prescription in Scotland' by Andrew Foyle
'A Practical Guide to the Construction and Rectification of Wills and Trust Instruments' by Edward Hewitt
'A Practical Guide to the Law of Bullying and Harassment in the Workplace' by Philip Hyland
'How to Be a Freelance Solicitor: A Practical Guide to the SRA-Regulated Freelance Solicitor Model' by Paul Bennett
'A Practical Guide to Prison Injury Claims' by Malcolm Johnson
'A Practical Guide to the Small Claims Track - 2nd Edition' by Dominic Bright
'A Practical Guide to Advising Clients at the Police Station' by Colin Stephen McKeown-Beaumont

'A Practical Guide to Antisocial Behaviour Injunctions' by Iain Wightwick
'Practical Mediation: A Guide for Mediators, Advocates, Advisers, Lawyers, and Students in Civil, Commercial, Business, Property, Workplace, and Employment Cases' by Jonathan Dingle with John Sephton
'The Mini-Pupillage Workbook' by David Boyle
'A Practical Guide to Crofting Law' by Brian Inkster
'A Practical Guide to Spousal Maintenance' by Liz Cowell
'A Practical Guide to the Law of Domain Names and Cybersquatting' by Andrew Clemson
'A Practical Guide to the Law of Gender Pay Gap Reporting' by Harini Iyengar
'A Practical Guide to the Rights of Grandparents in Children Proceedings' by Stuart Barlow
'NHS Whistleblowing and the Law' by Joseph England
'Employment Law and the Gig Economy' by Nigel Mackay & Annie Powell
'A Practical Guide to Noise Induced Hearing Loss (NIHL) Claims' by Andrew Mckie, Ian Skeate, Gareth McAloon
'An Introduction to Beauty Negligence Claims – A Practical Guide for the Personal Injury Practitioner' by Greg Almond
'Intercompany Agreements for Transfer Pricing Compliance' by Paul Sutton
'Zen and the Art of Mediation' by Martin Plowman
'A Practical Guide to the SRA Principles, Individual and Law Firm Codes of Conduct 2019 – What Every Law Firm Needs to Know' by Paul Bennett
'A Practical Guide to Adoption for Family Lawyers' by Graham Pegg
'A Practical Guide to Industrial Disease Claims' by Andrew Mckie & Ian Skeate
'A Practical Guide to Redundancy' by Philip Hyland
'A Practical Guide to Vicarious Liability' by Mariel Irvine
'A Practical Guide to Applications for Landlord's Consent and Variation of Leases' by Mark Shelton
'A Practical Guide to Relief from Sanctions Post-Mitchell and Denton' by Peter Causton
'A Practical Guide to Equity Release for Advisors' by Paul Sams
'A Practical Guide to Financial Services Claims' by Chris Hegarty

'The Law of Houses in Multiple Occupation: A Practical Guide to HMO Proceedings' by Julian Hunt
'Occupiers, Highways and Defective Premises Claims: A Practical Guide Post-Jackson – 2nd Edition' by Andrew Mckie
'A Practical Guide to Financial Ombudsman Service Claims' by Adam Temple & Robert Scrivenor
'A Practical Guide to Advising Schools on Employment Law' by Jonathan Holden
'A Practical Guide to Running Housing Disrepair and Cavity Wall Claims: 2nd Edition' by Andrew Mckie & Ian Skeate
'A Practical Guide to Holiday Sickness Claims – 2nd Edition' by Andrew Mckie & Ian Skeate
'Arguments and Tactics for Personal Injury and Clinical Negligence Claims' by Dorian Williams
'A Practical Guide to Drone Law' by Rufus Ballaster, Andrew Firman, Eleanor Clot
'A Practical Guide to Compliance for Personal Injury Firms Working With Claims Management Companies' by Paul Bennett
'RTA Allegations of Fraud in a Post-Jackson Era: The Handbook – 2nd Edition' by Andrew Mckie
'RTA Personal Injury Claims: A Practical Guide Post-Jackson' by Andrew Mckie
'On Experts: CPR35 for Lawyers and Experts' by David Boyle
'An Introduction to Personal Injury Law' by David Boyle
'A Practical Guide to Subtle Brain Injury Claims' by Pankaj Madan

These books and more are available to order online direct from the publisher at www.lawbriefpublishing.com, where you can also read free sample chapters. For any queries, contact us on 0844 587 2383 or mail@lawbriefpublishing.com.

Our books are also usually in stock at www.amazon.co.uk with free next day delivery for Prime members, and at good legal bookshops such as Wildy & Sons.

We are regularly launching new books in our series of practical day-to-day practitioners' guides. Visit our website and join our free newsletter to be kept informed and to receive special offers, free chapters, etc.

You can also follow us on Twitter at www.twitter.com/lawbriefpub.

www.ingramcontent.com/pod-product-compliance
Ingram Content Group UK Ltd.
Pitfield, Milton Keynes, MK11 3LW, UK
UKHW020151290926
15471UKWH00004B/809

9 781913 715687